Creative Juices Publishing

Made in the USA
Middletown, DE
13 December 2020

27602268R00062